Author: Callie Chapman
Illustrators: Bronwyne Chapman & Callie Chapman

Copyright © Callie Chapman, 2017

All rights reserved. No part of this book may be reproduced in any manner without written permission, except in the case of brief quotations embodied in critical articles and reviews.

ISBN 978-0-9973968-8-1

Glitter The Unicorn Goes to the Moon

By Callie Chapman

Seven-year-old Callie lives in Alabama with her family. This imaginative, smart, and funny girl came up with the story of Glitter the Unicorn and her best friend Ellie, named after her favorite stuffed animals. "Glitter the Unicorn Goes to the Moon" is the third book written by Callie following the adventures of Glitter the Unicorn and Ellie. Callie loves creating stories..so be on the lookout for more Glitter the Unicorn stories.

Glitter the Unicorn and Ellie board a pink and purple glittery rocket ship.

Glitter and Ellie sit in the front seat so they can see **space** outside the large window.

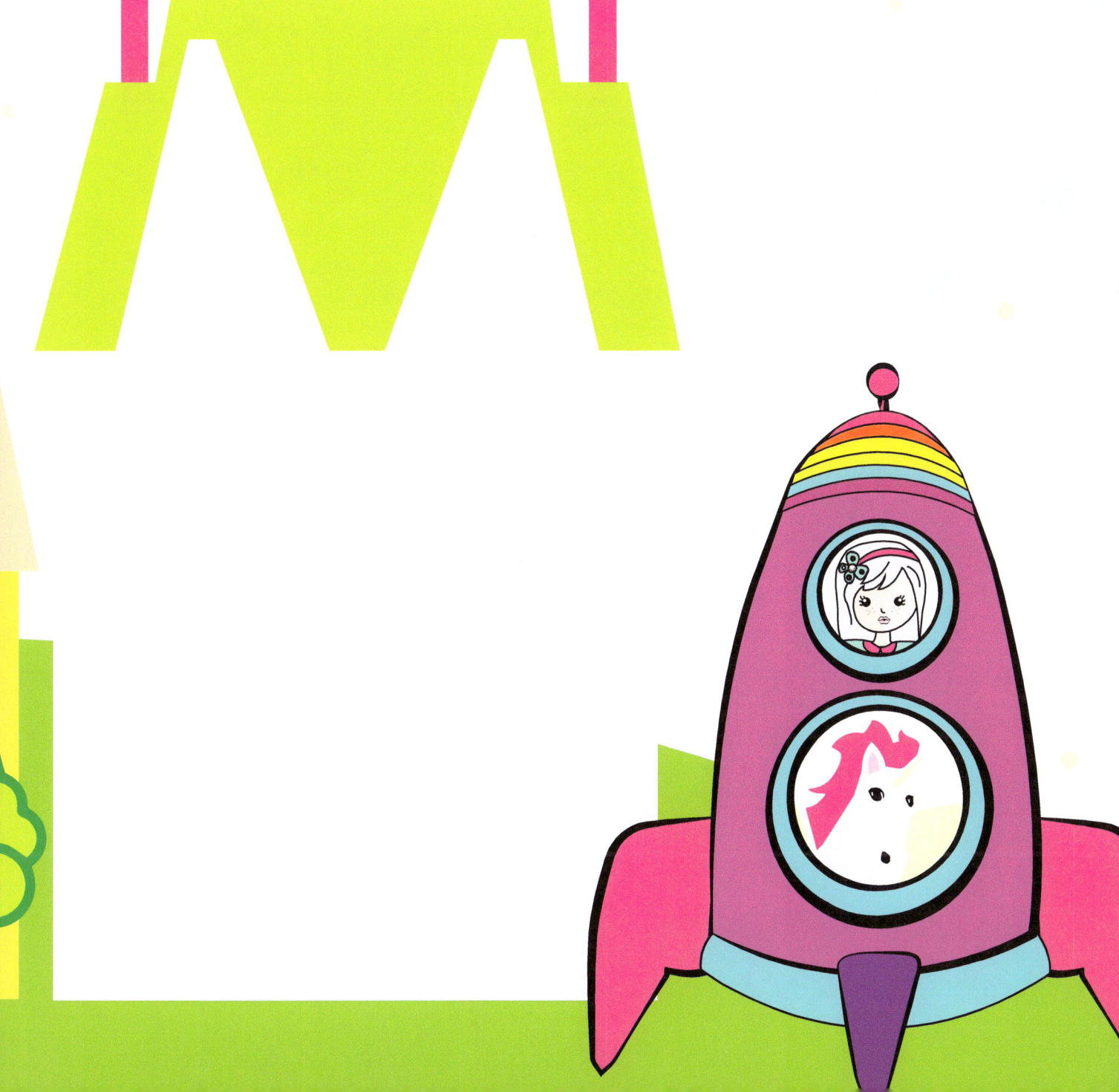

Glitter the Unicorn and Ellie find a castle made of moon rock hidden in a valley on the moon. Glitter and Ellie bounce and bounce toward the castle.

The Queen of the castle comes out to meet Glitter the Unicorn and Ellie. The Queen tells Glitter and Ellie that she Lost her magical crown.

The map shows Glitter and Ellie that they have to fish the ocean on Saturn for stars.

Glitter and Ellie find a **magical fishing rod** on the rocket ship.

Ellie casts the rod and catches **three stars.**
Ellie **keeps the stars** in her pocket.
Glitter and Ellie board the rocket ship.

To open the box, Glitter and Ellie will need **three stars** from the ocean on Saturn.

Ellie pulls the stars from her pocket and places the **stars on the box.**

Pow!!
An explosion of **Sparkly Moon Dust** zips through the air, and the box opens.

The shiny crown is inside.

Glitter the Unicorn and Ellie **thank** their **new friend** for all of her help. Glitter and Ellie board the rocket ship with the Queen's **sparkly crown**.

Glitter the Unicorn and Ellie fly **back to the moon**. Glitter and Ellie give the **magical crown** to the Queen.

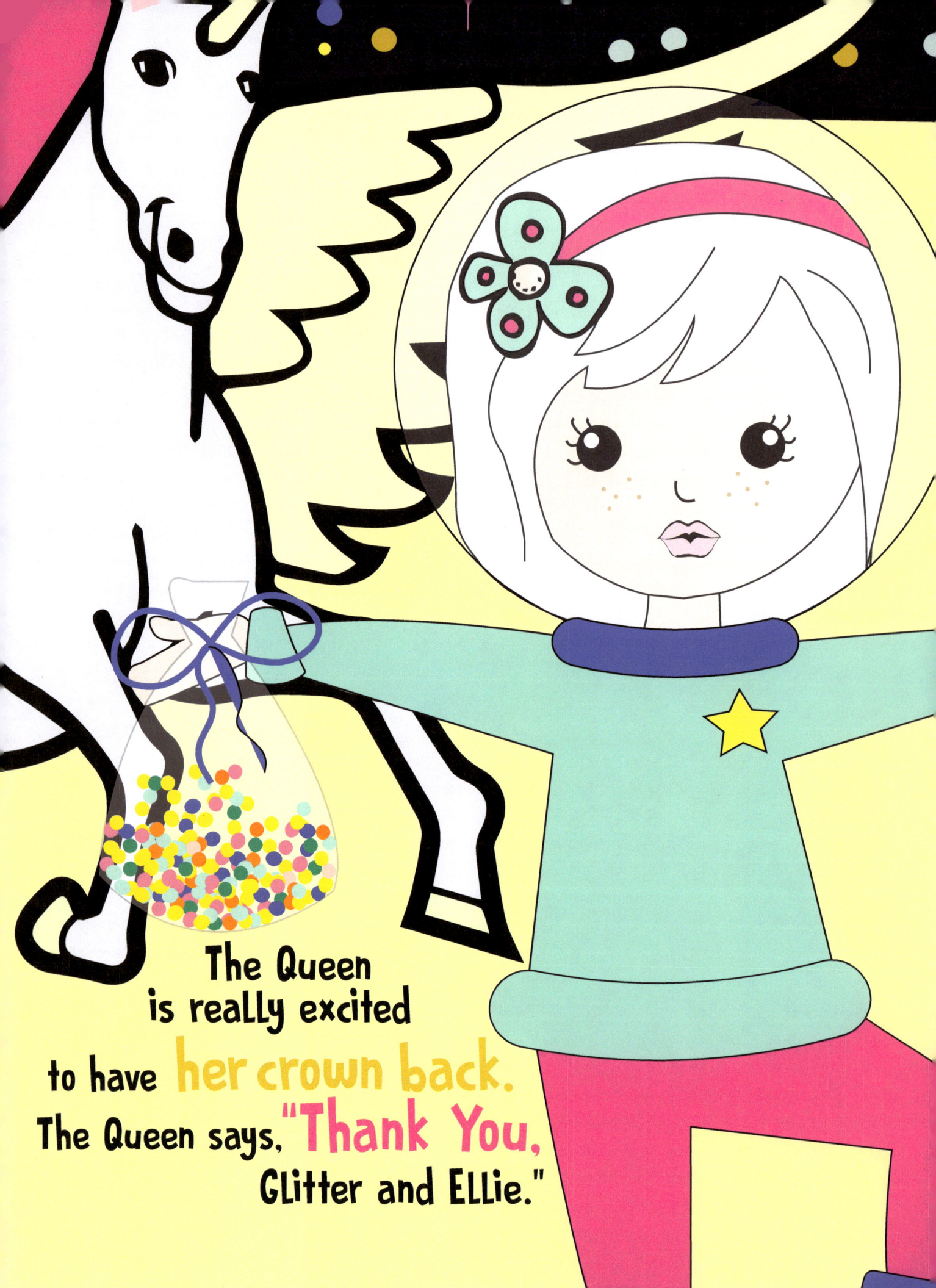

Glitter the Unicorn and Ellie **Loved** their adventure to the **moon** and their **new rock**.
This is the best birthday ever!

The End

Callie Chapman

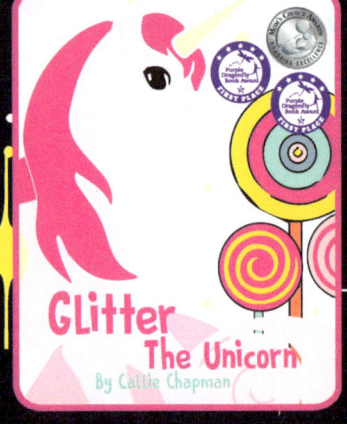
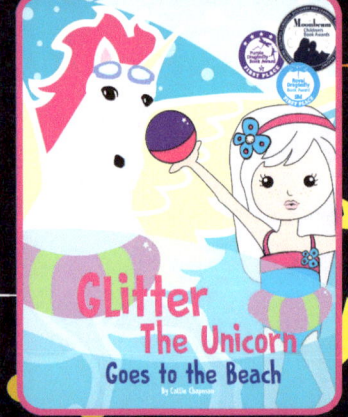

Glitter the Unicorn
Mom's Choice Award silver medal
1st Place Dragonfly Award
1st Place Purple Dragonfly Award
for best book series

Glitter the Unicorn Goes to the Beach
Moonbean Children's Award silver medal for best youth author
1st place Purple Dragonfly Award for best book series
1st place Royal Dragonfly Award for best interior design
HM Royal Dragonfly Award for best children's picture book

www.GlitterTheUnicorn.com

CPSIA information can be obtained
at www.ICGtesting.com
Printed in the USA
LVHW07n1614190318
570339LV00013B/408/P